Christian Evidence Serie

WHY PRAY?

by

Stephen Oliver

Rector of Leeds Parish Church

Published by The Canterbury Press Norwich
for the Christian Evidence Society

TO

HILARY, SIMON AND ADAM

WHO TAUGHT ME THE

WAY OF LIVING REFLECTIVELY

First published 1993 by The Canterbury Press Norwich
(a publishing imprint of Hymns Ancient & Modern Limited, a registered charity)
St Mary's Works, St Mary's Plain,
Norwich, Norfolk, NR3 3BH

British Library Cataloguing in Publication Data

A catalogue record for this book is available from the British Library

ISBN 1-85311-077-9

Typeset by Rowland Phototypesetting Limited
Bury St Edmunds, Suffolk
Printed and bound in Great Britain by
St Edmundsbury Press Limited
Bury St Edmunds, Suffolk

Why Pray?

So help me God

Prayer is primitive. That is to say it is a basic part of human experience. There is overwhelming evidence to show that on occasion people find themselves praying even when they don't consider themselves to be specially 'religious'.

When BBC Television investigated the disturbing safety record of ships at sea, Tom Mangold interviewed an officer from a bulk carrier which had gone down so suddenly that many of the crew had no time to escape. It was a harrowing story. The ship's hull had been so corroded that a gash opened up in the bow allowing the sea to pound mercilessly into the forward hold. Internal bulkheads fractured one after the other under the incessant pressure of the waves. Below the main deck only a thin wall stood between the engine room and the ocean when the order was given to abandon ship. The massive carrier sank in just six minutes. At this point Tom Mangold asked a direct but unusual question. 'Did you pray?' The officer, clearly moved, returned an equally direct answer. 'Yes, I prayed'.

Now a reporter of Tom Mangold's hardened experience isn't given to wasting valuable air-time by putting fatuous and irrelevant questions. He knew what he was doing. It wasn't enough to dig out the facts and list the number of ships lost at sea. It wasn't enough even to paint the picture of slack regulations and negligent owners out for a quick profit. If this programme was to be anything more than a passing story he had to reach the audience at that point where words alone can no longer express the anguish of human tragedy. In moments of ultimate crisis women and men pray! Who knows what fuelled that officer's prayer – fear for his life, grief for his friends – fury at the owners – anger at God? The point is that Tom Mangold knew the audience would identify with that officer precisely because in times of overwhelming catastrophe they too had found themselves praying.

It's easy to dismiss that kind of prayer as a last ditch attempt at self preservation. People do snatch at straws in a crisis and this experience of spontaneous prayers might be nothing more than the last shout of a misguided superstition. The trouble is that a personal crisis is very far from being the only situation which evokes this response of natural prayer. Nor is it by any means the case that self-preservation is the only motive for praying. On the contrary, the most urgent and immediate prayer is often for other people 'God help them'.

An experienced police officer was driving down the motorway listening to the sports programme on the afternoon of the tragic disaster at Hilsborough Football Stadium in Sheffield. The first reports were of people crushed and injured. Then followed accounts of supporters trapped inside the crowd barrier and soon it was clear that people had died. As the horror of that afternoon began to unfold he found himself pleading with God to help them. In his mind he could picture the stadium and knew that this was a major disaster. In so far as he was conscious of praying at all, he was aware that he held in that prayer the injured and dying, the emergency services and the families of the supporters waiting at home and worried sick. All this and more was contained in three words – 'God help them'. On reflection he was surprised at the fact that he found himself praying but it was so spontaneous he could not help himself.

Roy Williamson describes a similar experience in the aftermath of the fire at Bradford City football ground in 1985. The team had just won promotion to the Second Division of the Football League. It was a day of celebration which ended in tragedy when fire swept through the stand with ferocious speed leaving fifty six people dead. Early on Sunday morning a brief announcement on the local radio station let it be known that in the Cathedral later that day there would be an opportunity for people to come together and to pray. In the event the Cathedral was not only full to capacity but hundreds stood outside.

'It was an incredible testimony to people's need, in the face of inexplicable disaster and suffering, to be in touch with God – either to weep in sorrow or shake their fist in anger – and prayer was the way in.' (*Can You Spare a Minute*, Roy Williamson. DLT Daybreak 1991) The evidence suggests that at times of human crisis — (and particularly when it is other people who are involved) – it is not the case that people debate with themselves whether to pray. It is not even the case that people want to pray but rather that they need to pray. And that compelling experience is as natural as tears and as spontaneous as laughter.

In fact there are no limits to the range of occasions when spontaneous prayer comes as a natural response riding on the emotions but directed to God. Joy and happiness, relief, thankfulness or sheer *joie de vie* – a sense of exuberance and delight can be carriers of that surge of prayer. John Emery was surprised by that unexpected moment when it came to him at the end of a difficult climb.

'Later when I came to the harder routes, I found something else, a new state of mind. This was a sudden and overwhelmingly powerful sensation of humility and gratitude, so real that I could only interpret it as being directed towards a creator. I had never been able to arrive at such a conviction through a process of reason, yet here I was forced to accept it, despite myself . . . I had made no conscious effort to achieve it; there was no act of contemplation. It just happened when I was coiling up the rope at the end of a climb; as prosaic as that.' (*The Alpine Journal* 1961 Nov. 'The Runcible Cat')

In a very different context the French composer Hector Berlioz was surprised by that unexpected moment whilst listening to music.

'The sound filled me with a passionate unrest from which I was powerless to hide. I saw heaven open – purer and a thousand times lovelier than the one that had so often been described to me. Such is the incomparable beauty of melody that comes from the heart.' (*Memoirs of Hector Berlioz*, Gollancz 1969).

Spontaneous prayer of this kind which springs up in response to a range of human experiences is very far from being self indulgent or egocentric. On the contrary such instinctive prayer is often the profound expression of concern for the well being of others. It can also arise as a sense of deep thankfulness in the face of astonishing beauty or well up from an overwhelming feeling of awe at the sheer mystery of life in the birth of a baby.

One other experience can be the context in which prayer is born but it attracts less attention today than in the past. It is an important if neglected part of human nature and because it can be a painful area it is too often avoided. To be human is to take a high measure of responsibility for oneself and a care for others. People are also sinners who know what it is to fail and what it is to be guilty of wrong doing. There are occasions for most people when punishment and retaliation have been deserved, but instead of that they have been met with kindness and understanding. That experience of guilt and grace in relation to God is to come up against what Graham Greene described as 'the appalling strangeness of the mercy of God'. It is that mysterious moment when forgiveness is sought and graciously given. The desire for forgiveness and the gift of grace meet in consciousness at the point of prayer.

In all these areas of human experience where prayer is an instinct rather than a deliberate decision the overwhelming feeling is that of being taken out of yourself. It is a moment however fleeting when thankfulness, or desire and yearning – whatever it might be – is directed to God. Yet what makes it all so hard to put into words is the fact that this experience of prayer hardly reaches the level of language at all.

> ‘ . . . And prayer is more
> Than an order of words, the conscious occupation
> Of the praying mind, or the sound of the voice praying.’
>
> (‘Little Gidding’ a poem by T.S. Eliot,
> in *Selected Poems*, Faber 1954)

Many people will recognise the experience of such prayer even if they lay no claim to formal religious belief and even if their hold on the very notion of God is somewhat tenuous.

Why pray? Because at times it is such a fundamental part of our nature that it is instinctive. Because uniquely it conveys however haltingly the deepest concerns and the greatest delights of our life. Because at this primitive, basic level of prayer if we did not pray we would not be human.

Say one for me

Prayer is dangerous. On the negative side there is always the temptation to pander to the immature demands of the child within. This is one reason why prayer is often reduced to the level of ‘asking for things’. It is not that prayers in this mode are wrong. The problem is that they have not evolved into a much wider and deeper experience. Children are taught quite rightly to pray in this fashion, but then later their spiritual growth is stunted. The inevitable result is that an adult person is saddled with an immature spirituality. Hardly surprising then that the demands of the child inside should become expressed as prayer to the great God somewhere outside. When such demands are not clearly met then of course prayer is said to be a waste of time.

The reality of prayer, however, is more complex and much more interesting. In fact since prayer is the ‘way in’ to a conscious relationship with God it cannot be less interesting than what might be observed in any personal human relationship.

All human relationships are a mixture of motives and needs but there is no denying that the most authentic relationships are found where people affirm one another. By contrast, the most fragile relationships in business, marriage or community are those based on exploitation. In other words people in mature relationships are there because they want to be there not primarily for what they can get out of it. Now in this context it must be said that prayer invoked as a 'magic formula' or prayer intended as a means of divine manipulation will not work! Such prayer only reinforces the wrong kind of immature dependence.

In the north transept of York Minster myriad numbers of candles cast a warm glow over the cold stones. The modern pilgrim is invited to light a candle as a prayer. It would be easy to dismiss this invitation as pandering to the immature superstitions of vulnerable visitors. But nearby is a notice which spells out with commendable brevity how authentic prayer is always a mature expression of concern for others or a heightened response to a transcendent truth. Prayer takes you out of yourself, it doesn't lock you in. The notice read:

> 'You are invited to light a candle as a prayer:
> In response to beauty and goodness
> In thought for others
> As an offering of oneself.'

The Christian faith is quite clear that whilst we are dependent on God as the 'whence of our being', that is for our very existence, nonetheless God *relates* to us with respect for our freedom and by affirming each individual's personhood. Respect for freedom and affirming ultimate worth are the two most significant ingredients in any creative relationship that has the potential for growth. That is why the most profound prayers are not the longest but the most perceptive. They start not with pleading but with affirmation:

> 'The Lord is my shepherd . . .'
> 'Our Father in heaven . . .'
> 'God of grace and God of glory . . .'

And they end with respect for the sovereign, freedom of God trusting that in freedom God will do what is good:

> '. . . yet not my will but thine be done'
> '. . . Lord hear us. Lord graciously hear us.'
> '. . . for the kingdom, the power and the glory
> are yours now and forever.'

Prayer that starts here has the potential power to enable people to grow in their perceptions and in their personality. Only one other ingredient is required – honesty! No relationship will ever flower without it. The agnostic's cry for help – 'O God if there is a God, save my soul if I've got one' might not reach the heights of literary achievement but it certainly stands on the bedrock of authentic prayer. As does St Augustine's famous plea 'God make me chaste – but not yet'.

The uncomfortable aspect of this honest, affirming prayer is its capacity to boomerang back. It is hard (to the point of hypocrisy) to call God Father, yet secretly believe that people of a different class, creed or colour are not also your own brothers and sisters. Far from being an innocent pastime, prayer can be a dangerous threat to all manner of personal and political prejudices. But then growing into a new maturity always was a risky business!

> 'Prayer is not an old woman's idle amusement.
> Properly understood and applied it is the
> most potent instrument of action'
>
> Gandhi

Why pray? Because it would be unfortunate to say the least to reach sixty with the spiritual understanding of a six year old.

Prayer is dangerous. On the positive side it is about the willingness to be open – to new truth – to yourself – to other people. The Dutch poet and priest Huub Oosterhuis expressed this vulnerable openness in a prayer of his own.

'Lord our God . . .
make us receptive
to everything you can give us.'

Never mind the prayers that ask for this and that. What does God want to give? Divine respect for human freedom means that nothing can be given that is not willingly received. That is the significance of the way in which Jesus of Nazareth taught his followers how to pray:

> 'Do not heap up empty phrases as the Gentiles do; they think that they will be heard for their many words. Your Father knows what you need before you ask him so then pray like this:
>
> Our Father in heaven . . .'
>
> Matthew 6.7

God cannot give what is needed if a person is not open to receive it. Prayer is asking to receive.

If the Bible is to be believed then God wants to give all manner of good things to his children, save that their freedom to accept or reject those things will always be respected. The problem in the western world is that people are bombarded by all sorts of peer group aspirations, advertising publicity and political slogans. It is not at all clear that we know what we need even though we may have been convinced that we know what we want. Not that the problem is a new one. Two thousand five hundred years ago one of the ancient Jewish prophets was making a similar plea on behalf of his people:

'Give me a pure heart O God
and put a right spirit within me.'

The first priority of prayer is to know what we need, to see clearly what is required. It is an experience of heightened perception. A psychiatrist once justified his expensive fee by asking his client – 'How do you know what you think until you tell me?' It may sound an odd question but it's true to experience. Someone asks at a dinner party, 'what do you think about Capital Punishment?' There is silence except for the meshing of mental gears as people genuinely work out what they do think about it. Then occasionally they surprise themselves since they had never expressed a view on the question before. Prayer is the opportunity for that kind of self awareness to grow but it demands a risky openness that can be quite disturbing.

In this sense prayer is not unlike the experience of talking to yourself. But there is a real difference. Every summer during the Wimbledon Tennis tournament players are heard talking to themselves with words of biting criticism or energised encouragement. To talk to yourself like that leads nowhere beyond the present moment – or worse. Shut up inside yourself the conversation finally runs into the sand. The experience of prayer is very different precisely because the underlying intention is to be open and receptive so that there is always the possibility for some new perception to grow, some new insight to be grasped, some new possibility to be seen.

Ultimately prayer is an attempt to be open more fully to that direct communion with God that is revealed in the lives of those spiritual giants of faith. To pray compassionately led Albert Schweitzer to give up his brilliant academic career to live in Africa caring for lepers. Prayer for the terminally ill led Cicely Saunders to establish a modern hospice much as prayer 'for the despis'd slave' led William Wilberforce down the road which led to the abolition of trade in human beings.

Prayer is dangerous because when it is truly open then God knows what might happen next! To return to the question about whether prayer works then the honest answer is no, if prayer is exercised as a magic formula or intended as a selfish manipulation of people or events. But if the question is asked 'Does prayer make a difference?' then the unequivocal answer has to be yes. Prayer makes a discernible difference to the one who prays and in my experience a profound difference to the subject held in that prayer. Yet there is certainly no easy connection of cause and effect, no telepathic instrument to satisfy the mystery of this divine communion. Why pray? Because the conviction grows with praying that this is the most profound contribution that can be made in the realm of our deepest concerns, not as a substitute for thought or action but as the unique means of undergirding and inspiring both. To pray for others in their need is often the only thing that can be done. It is also a very personal thing to do. And those who are held in prayer often express a profound gratitude even if they do not pray for themselves.

You'll never walk alone

The exercise of prayer is a journey of discovery. It requires an element of trust and that trust can only grow with experience. Michael Novak makes the point that 'it is in prayer that one comes to know God best'. He goes on to ask the intriguing question as to whether people do not pray because they do not believe in God, or whether they do not believe in God because they have never learned to pray? (*Belief and Unbelief*, Macmillan 1966).

To pray is to concentrate in such a relaxed yet focused way that ever deeper layers of reality are revealed and ever more nuances of truth are discovered in people and in the world. Faith's name for the ultimate reality and the source of truth is God. To rest in God and to stay with God is to pray.

Instinctive prayer which springs from a particular experience as a response to God is both natural and biblical. Natural because it is so common in widely different cultures and times; biblical because there is such a strong tradition in the scriptures of Judaism and Christianity that prayer is what God enables to happen.

> 'When we cry "Abba – Father!" – it is the Spirit of God bearing witness with our spirit that we are children of God.
>
> 'The Spirit helps us in our weakness; for we do not know how to pray . . . but the Spirit intercedes for us with sighs too deep for words.'
>
> (St Paul's Letter to the Romans 8)

Communion with God which is the essence of prayer is also God's gift. But it always remains a gift that can be refused, abused or ignored.

The starting point in developing prayer beyond the instinctive urge evoked by a particular situation is to have the courage to pray. In a secular society with no apparent need for God, old habits of thought die hard. It is not easy to recognise those deeper rhythms of life that have been ironed out by a consumer society. It takes courage to resist the brainwashing which dismissed prayer as meaningless, but then people in other ages also thought like that, only to discover again its curious attraction.

'What profit do we get if we pray?' (Job 21) is a slogan which finds an astonishing echo in a world which asks 'what's in it for me?' There comes a point where effort is required to combat the spiritual bankruptcy which fosters a corrosive cynicism eating away at questions of value, purpose and meaning.

Once the breakthrough has been made then patience is needed to recover those skills of waiting, stillness and concentration that have been wasting away. The evidence of those who have trodden this path suggests that at some point there comes the experience of being met and accompanied on the journey. This is not to say that there will be no times of dryness – a dark night of the soul and a feeling of emptiness. In one sense this is only to be expected. An athlete in training goes through a similar period when progress seems hard. Relationships go through barren times only to flourish again later. The trick is not to panic but to persevere.

When that first step has been taken, then the journey begins to have about it the element of discovery. Others too have been here and left the marks of their passing.

If honesty, for example, is required as a vital ingredient in the practice of prayer then the language of the ancient Psalms knows no bounds in telling God straight.

> 'why do you stand far off O Lord
> Why do you hide your face in time of need?'
> Ps 10
>
> 'When I slipped they mocked me:
> and gnashed at me with their teeth.
> Lord how long will you look on?' Ps 35
>
> 'As the deer longs for the running brooks
> so longs my soul for you O God.' Ps 42
>
> 'O God the heathen have come into your land
> we have become a mockery to our neighbours
> the scorn and laughing stock of those about us.'
> Ps 79
>
> 'O God you know my foolishness
> And my sins are not hidden from you. Ps 69

Old and young, sinner and saint, heathen and destitute – all manner of life and every human emotion is carried in those honest and open prayers.

But emotional incontinence is not altogether the most creative channel of prayer though it is often a cathartic experience that can clear away a lot of rubbish.

The time comes however when honest prayer needs to be focused but not censored.

Jesus of Nazareth had to teach his followers this art of spiritual concentration. There are many stories which convey his own rhythm of prayer and the vital importance he attached to it. He is reported as going into the hills to be alone to pray without distraction. Exhaustion makes concentration difficult but the immensity of the landscape and the nearness of the stars can help to bring the presence of God back into focus. It is after a period of intense activity that Jesus is often found to be alone or praying with his closest friends. He regularly visited the Temple and on one occasion insisted to the point of physical confrontation that it should be a house of prayer. Sometimes his prayer could be a silent thanksgiving as he broke the bread that fed the people on a lonely hillside or an anguished cry as in the Garden of Gethsemane when 'his sweat like drops of blood fell down upon the ground'.

The important legacy he left is not so much rhythm of his prayers as the pattern of prayer with which he taught his followers.

Until recently it was the one prayer that everyone in Christendom knew by heart. Today there is a confusion of forms and not everyone is taught it at school even in a nominal Christian country. It may be that future generations will discover it with delight having hardly known it in their youth.

The prayer begins with phrases of affirmation and honour:

> 'Our Father in heaven
> hallowed by your name.'

From the very start the prayer conveys a note of intimacy and trust.

Then follows the first petition:

'Your kingdom come
Your will be done
on earth as in heaven.'

At first it appears to be such a nebulous request. Why not pray for food, housing or employment? The point is that authentic prayer deals first with the ultimate issues not just the symptoms of human concern. Take for example the evil of famine which has been so endemic in parts of the world like Somalia and Ethiopia. Over the years the failure of crops and the poverty of the people have not been the factors which fermented the famine into such a deathly catastrophe. It was the savage civil war which consumed vital resources and finally condemned children and mothers, young men and old people to a fatal starvation.

Food given by the aid agencies was hijacked before it could be distributed. Fighting between rival gangs prevented access to the interior villages. What the situation needed more than food was a revolution in human affairs that would allow the supplies to get through. When Jesus taught his followers to pray for the Kingdom of God, it was for a transformation of that blind wickedness which has allowed evil to wreak such death and destruction. Whenever people are locked into a vicious circle by prejudice, fear and hatred in Bosnia, Serbia, Sri Lanka or Northern Ireland the priority prayer must be for the coming of the Kingdom, the rule of God. It could not be expressed more precisely than in this prayer.

Having said that it must be added that prayer which never includes any particularities will also lack any real engagement with the profound issues of the world. To that extent the prayer of Jesus needs to be 'earthed' in the concerns of the moment. But then the prayer itself never gives any excuse for a religious flight of fantasy. There is nothing more 'earthy' than to pray for bread.

'Give us today our daily bread.' It is a straightforward prayer that can be used with great simplicity.

But it also carries an elusive depth of meaning. In practice it is one of the most difficult phrases to translate from the Greek of the Christian gospels. In the days before supermarket shopping a family would go to the local bakery and place an order for tomorrow's bread. When there were no deep freezers and bread went stale in a very short time, it was important to have fresh bread regularly supplied. Somewhere in this prayer for daily bread is the request that God might provide tomorrow's fresh bread – today. It is another way of expressing a longing for the Kingdom of God which is yet to come.

But that Kingdom can only be given when it is willingly received. So the prayer moves on to confront those barriers which prevent the coming of the Kingdom.

> 'Forgive us our sins
> As we forgive those who sin against us.'

Once again there is a realism here which cannot be avoided. The healing of God's forgiveness is gladly and generously offered with the one provision that such forgiveness should spill over into the healing of every fractured human relationship. There is evidence in the teaching of Jesus that divine forgiveness even precedes the expression of penitence. Jesus accepts the tax collector Zacheus and goes to his home even before Zacheus confesses his faults. The Father of the Prodigal Son rushes out to meet him before the penitent lad has chance to utter a word. There are no conditions laid down to qualify for God's forgiveness, save that when it is received it should be shown to others in the same generous spirit.

The prayer of Jesus finally confronts the ultimate issue of evil. The famous psychiatrist Carl Jung used to complain that theologians never took evil seriously enough. The same cannot be said of Jesus!

'Lead us not into temptation' is a pointed prayer for deliverance when faith is tested, confidence is eroded and evil is confronted. It is the test that Jesus faced in the wilderness and more acutely in the Garden of Gethsemane. It is the climax of the prayer and the most crucial petition.

The prayer ends with a final acclamation of glory which includes an expression of trust and faith:

'For the Kingdom, the power and the glory
are yours now and forever. Amen.'

This prayer has been handed down from generation to generation. Saints and sinners have been instructed by it in every age. Sometimes the prayers of the past seem more of an encumbrance on the journey of faith rather than a help. To use them seems at times like trying to walk in boots that are several sizes too big. But the point is not to be intimidated by them. Rather than abandon them altogether it is worthwhile considering whether in time you might just grow into them. The Lord's Prayer is a prayer that will from time to time be the channel of fresh insight and new spiritual growth.

Why pray? Because at rock bottom four thousand years of evolutionary history have been invested in human beings who have learned how to pray. It would be foolish to settle for our own spiritual desert when previous generations have discovered the odd lush pasture and green oasis. Those generations might not have had the knowledge that is enjoyed in our age but without their spiritual depth, our knowledge could prove more of a threat than a promise to the future.

Pray up and shut up

Prayer is more – far more than words. When I was growing up my grandparents lived just down the street. They never locked their front door which shows how different life was in those days. I could go in and see them whenever I liked and no doubt there were times when they were glad to see the back of me. But I remember very clearly walking down the street and thinking what a good idea it would be to surprise them if I crept into the house without them knowing that I was coming! It was a dark early evening in winter. They still had gas lights in their house and an open fire in the hearth. As I crept down the hall, I heard nothing but the creak of a rocking chair, the hiss of the gas mantle and the odd dropping of ash from the fire into the grate. I stood for a while outside the living room door, caught in a companionable silence. Both my grandfather and grandmother had got to the stage where words weren't that important any more. They enjoyed simply being together. In the end, I couldn't bring myself to shatter that stillness so I crept out, waited a while and then went back with my usual clod hopping step and shouted down the hallway 'It's only me'.

There comes a point where prayer is more like a companionable silence than a frantic conversation. It is best described as an awareness of God – a walking with God all the time rather than paying the occasional visit. Of course it is vital to attend to prayer, setting time aside, being alone and so on. But those times come to inform the whole of life rather than be excursions from an otherwise busy schedule.

Why pray? Because life is more than a superficial existence. At the end of the day questions of purpose and meaning and value will only be answered, however haltingly, from a depth that comes from reflective living.

Faith and hope and love – the great spiritual gifts have to be nurtured and developed. Like any other human attribute they need to be used and exercised. In the end they are fed from that reflective living in the consciousness of God that is called prayer.